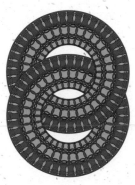

Against Consolation

Books by
ROBERT CORDING

POETRY

Life-list (1987)
What Binds Us to This World (1991)
Heavy Grace (1996)

EDITED

In My Life: Encounters with the Beatles (1998)
(eds: Cording, Jankowski-Smith, Miller-Laino)

Against Consolation

ROBERT CORDING

CavanKerry ◊ Press Ltd.

Library of Congress Cataloging-in-Publication Data

Cording, Robert.
    Against consolation / by Robert Cording.
        p. cm.
    ISBN 0-9678856-9-8
        I. Title.
    PS3553.O6455 A73 2001
    811'.54—dc21

                                    2001042504

Cover painting by Robert Dente: A Pond In Rain
Cover and text design by Sylvia Frezzolini Severance

First Edition

CavanKerry Press Ltd
Fort Lee, New Jersey
www.cavankerrypress.com

— for Robert, Daniel, and Thomas
and in memory of Robert Creevy

What can I know? What should I do? What may I hope?

—Immanuel Kant,
Critique of Pure Reason

Contents

Three

Against Consolation

One

Mappings

I

A ship crossing the cold space of a sea
and, along the deck, a man walking
who every so often turns as if he believes
there is something ahead in the grey
although there is just the flat expanse
of the sea. It is morning, the year 1913,
the ship four hundred miles west
of Greenland's northern tip and he
is waiting for what he expects will be
the outlines of a land put on a map
seven years earlier. When two mountains
then four shoulder through the mist,
their nameless procession rising from
the sea, he sees that valleys and rivers
must be part of their topography
and imagines brooks of clear water rushing
over smoothed purple stones, the scents
of spring grasses, and a covey of ptarmigans
weaving in and out of sight, a lightness
in their flurries of quick, whistled calls.

II

But now is the hour when the glistening
mountains unravel like expectations,
replaced by the sea's ennui of lift and fall.
He writes in his log: *Peary's island is a mirage*.

And yet, within this very hour, the island
appears again, the mountains floating up
like clouds, their lost, familiar landscape
regained as the ship sails off. He watches
his crew shake their heads and joke easily
among themselves, then bend once more
to their tasks, and feels contempt
for his need to inhabit this bleakest of seas;
he cannot help but marvel at how the sea,
without a will, simply creates what is
entirely missing, a world he finds impossible
to let go of, even if he knows these mountains
leaning towards him so beautifully and their
quick, snowmelt creeks threading the landscape—
their banks printed with plovers and caribou,
with raccoon, marten, and fox—are not there.

Elegy for Chris McCandless

> After graduating from college, Chris McCandless
> gave the remainder of his tuition fund, over $24,000,
> to OXFAM to fight hunger and journeyed to Alaska
> in order to fulfill his goal of being "lost in the wild."
> He died of starvation.

Between the river moving in ice-
bordered pools of black water
and the forest warped in
early snow, he slipped away.

His mother on the other side
of the country knew it
was too late, always too late
to save him. He could not live

in the world in the usual way.
What others wanted was too little—
mutual acceptance that shrugs
and says, the poor are always

with us, then goes on counting
its blessings. What could he do
once he recognized the *false
being* within him? He began

to walk towards the clean slate
of the woods where stars
sharpen themselves in wide spaces
of sky and the body breathes

in the certain knowledge
of air's steel blade. He chose
another name, gave away his money,
wrote across a W-4 form:

Exempt, Exempt, Exempt.
Because so many went hungry,
he gave up eating, his one companion
the moon, starving itself

in quarters and eighths.
Who can say why he refused
to turn back? It's said the spirit
chooses its own affliction,

as he chose to become a figure
of himself in a photograph,
a last self-portrait of a man
smiling for a camera:

seventy-three pounds,
he spreads his arms wide
in a world entirely desolate.
Overhead, storms of light

and what may be a hawk changing
itself to smoke and wind,
disappearing over Denali's edge
as autumn flashes across Alaska

in premature cold. Such
a headstrong wish to be free

of everything, even his body's
twenty-four years. Some believe

he came to know the ecstasy
of dispossession, poor enough
in the end to slip through
a needle's eye. We do not know

if he was happy or afraid
at the end. Both, or neither.
We know only that he was found
wrapped in a sleeping bag

his mother had sewn for him;
that he sat at the window
of a bus, Fairbanks Transit 42,
as if he were a commuter returning

home from work. But the bus wasn't
moving. It was left as
a makeshift shelter along a river
that threaded miles of spruce.

He leaned his head against
the window, watching perhaps
as the ghost-mist of his breath
spread across the glass.

Then he was gone. The stars
went on, and the snow-fed river,
and the snow that drifted against
the bus. His body was found—

starved, frozen, preserved—
like someone from another age
buried under years of ice, the clues
we collect a means of explaining

the circumstances of his death,
though there's no giving voice
to the man, so like ourselves,
who went off and never returned.

Self-Portrait

So strongly present, enclosed
in familiar features: all you
ever see, your self, unreal
to the Buddhist monk, but
something you cannot get rid of.

Inconceivable, this face, yours
just once to wear, that says, *You
can go this far and no further.*
That grins, self-mockingly,
when you try to reach with words'

tenuous liaisons what you believe
words do not invent.
Your petitions repeat themselves,
endlessly trying to get it right,
but still you hear only

your own voice, your will
never strong enough
to will nothing. So here
you are, fleshed out in features
that tell the same old story

year after year, the end
just beginning to make itself
clear in the bony ridges
rising to the surface
of your cheeks, in the deep

holes into which your eyes
stare, and sink, an emptiness
asking, *What have you ever seen*
beyond the point of vanishing
to which we have brought you?

In My Study

An earthen pot of the Acoma,
    its yin-yang of black and white
        working against the one way pull of time.

A cone from a 4,000 year old
        Bristlecone pine. Stones and shells
        scattered on tables, like hieroglyphs

for which I have no code.
        Feathers from a yellow-shafted flicker—
            all that remained around a ring of blood

on the spring grass. Nests
    of phoebes and swallows that lived
        in the cool shadows of the barn's rafters

or along the ledges of our windows
    where the unrevisable days disappear
        and start again. And one—

a warbler's?—of delicately woven grass,
        housed in a talcum powder box.
            A gift, proof of a summer's love.

Her hair was dark and wiry,
        her brown eyes large and round.
            Inside the box, the strong fresh scent

of talcum. Almost the smell
        of her bare shoulders. On the mantle,
                a carved wren, small fluent singer

that gives the marsh a voice,
        though its song is sung with nothing
                in mind. And a catfish's skullbone—

shaped like a crucifix
        for those who can believe
                each thing is more than what it is.

And, in a chimney cupboard,
        a box of cast lead musicians
                I once arranged and rearranged—

a small boy's music, heard
        beyond concern in the mind's
                sweetest reverie. Objects

I've collected and cared for,
        loved and worried over, their loss
                something I have tried to prevent.

How could I believe,
        still believe, they can name
                what it means to exist here?

When I am gone, someone
        will throw them away
                or sell them, or take them

to another house like this one
    where thresholds and bannisters
        have been carved and smoothed

by the feet and hands
    of inhabitants who lived once
        and were never known again.

Distances

Outside her window, afternoon sun
stretches the shadows of Sunday
visitors, mostly middle-aged children
who push their mothers and fathers
in wheelchairs down a walkway
that disappears at a bend in the distance
like a child's unimaginable view
of the future. Your mother is talking,
a childhood memory of a Sunday drive
up a two-lane mountain road.
It's early spring, crab-apple trees
half-white with blossoms, fresh greens
watercoloring the roadside trees,
blue sky, gleaming white clouds.
She stops abruptly, as if the day's
particulars, so intact and real
moments before, had become
substanceless. When she begins again,
it's at a turn in the road. *Suddenly,*
she says, *we came upon a little restaurant*
with red and white striped awnings
and outside tables where a wedding dinner
was taking place. The tables were filled
with uncarved roasts and steaming platters
of potatoes and vegetables.
We catch her excitement, and see
for a moment the man standing
to give a toast, the glass so perfectly
transparent in the focused sun

it seems he's holding a medallion of light.
Then, she says, *just as suddenly*
as the wedding appeared, it vanished,
our car entering a long tunnel.
When we came out, we were higher up,
on the mountain's other side
where the trees were still leafless.
We want more, but your mother,
tired now, can only recall the strangeness
of seeing the bride who was
being toasted half in tears and yet smiling
and lovely, an image now seventy years old,
the tangible fullness of a moment
bearing down on us in all its final unreality.

Between Worlds

At the room's threshold you paused
as if caught by the stillness at the heart
of grief's sheer drop and, like Vermeer's
woman holding up her empty scales
in the window's light, you held the room's
remote self-containment: the sadness
of failing light at the windows; the few
things no longer his—a ring of keys,
a wallet, some prayer books; the lamp
and clock on the side table; the rented
hospital bed, stripped now, that waited
like a bed in some halfway house
between worlds where the dying sift
through the last certainties that prop up
their lives, and then are gone, leaving
the dumbstruck living to weigh
an unthinkable life, a death, an empty room.

The Purse

As if everything she needed to save herself
were within her reach and all she had to do
was piece together the clues inside
her purse, she hovers over the kitchen table
like some necromancer, hour by hour
removing combs and loose coins, a set of keys,
glasses and a compact, shiny lipstick cases,
a wallet of pictures, each thing held up
to the light the way a child holds up the world's
strangeness, and then placed on the table,
arranged and rearranged, her children
and grandchildren laid out like a tarot deck,
the coins and keys like compass points.
Her son can plead, *no mom, please, please stop;*
he can pray for a God to come and in one
pure word restore his mother's stricken brain;
he can whisper, *I love you,* meaning
I don't know what to do anymore, but he cannot
take the purse from his mother who carries it
to the bathroom and sleeps with it by her side.
He cannot understand why his mother,
lost now in the same world in which she knew
every turn of the local roads, keeps mapping
that trail of lipstick cases and keys
not even she can read; nor why, after thinking
has ended, after each of her efforts
satisfies nothing, the mind keeps following
its ever-restless hunger for some
incomprehensible and inexpressible order.

Questions

I often watched you praying, amazed
by how your mind righted itself
as you spoke, the broken world collected
in your murmuring voice, in words
which found the path through the maze
of disconnections your brain had become,

and asked myself whether your mind
(so much already stricken from memory)
fixed on the easy requirements of rote;
or if those words were the impress of your God's
burning seal, your own mind long given
to the relinquishments of prayer; or if, simply,
the words themselves were what you held to,
whatever world was left, living and meaning in them.

Nests

More than we imagined,
visible now that we can see
through the leafless branches—

nests, in the lilacs, near
the trunk of a weeping cherry,
on a maple branch horizon.

In them, the past
summer: dead grasses,
milkweed and dandelion

down, our lost cat's
white fur, line I cut
from a fishing reel, bits

of scattered fingernail-
sized eggshells—a robin's
pale blue and, the color

of century-old photographs,
with spots of two shades
of brown on cream, the remains

of a phoebe's eggs. Over
seven days in June, 1855,
Thoreau filled a journal

with quick jottings on tens
of nests—date, place,
type—as he tried to teach

his eyes to *saunter,* to celebrate
without ordering what was
gathered from odds and ends

and sown here and there
like the random matter of creation.
We try, too, but find ourselves

looking at these nests as if they
were old letters or diaries
that conceal as much as they

confide about a world
scattered with bits of narrative,
a story we cannot quite tell

and cannot keep from telling.

Narcissus

On this first day
of July it should be
adequate to walk here
in this hour's
casual articulations
of color and shadow
without fret of words
to catch the substance
of the short-lived
yellow of daylilies
after rain, or splashes
of light pearled
on the refreshed grass.
But at the pond, water
lilies have come up
for air, ripe
for symbol: pure white,
they hold out
their cupped hands
for blessings of light,
their roots far below,
sunk in black muck.
Nymphaea, from
an old fable we needed
to warn ourselves with—
the object of our
imaginings the beautiful
nymph who must hide
from our greedy eyes

in the flower's form.
Now a phoebe
wags its tail, as if
in recognition, and
lets go its two notes
which I can't help hearing
as its given name.
And now, in shifts
of wind, seeds
of tallest grasses
take wing. Aimless,
they fly to wherever
the wind will root them.
I have reached
my destination and,
kneeling at water's edge,
look and see myself
framed by everything
that goes on
endlessly beginning.

Gift

How carefully he unwrapped it
from his handkerchief—as if it were a relic
and not the skullbone

of a Florida sailcat, a sham
trinket for tourists who'd like a story to tell,
another legend of the true

cross or of a world revealing
itself in signs that say there's always something
underneath: boil the catfish's

thin sill of flesh away
and the reticulate bone beneath is revealed
as the crucifix it was meant to be.

Shake the cross, and hear
the storied dice cast for Christ's garments.
At first glance, I saw the cross,

even the body hanging there,
outstretched. But where the loving face
of Christ should have been

there was only some bony
voodoo conjunction of a ram's curled horns,
an alligator's toothy grin—

a sign, I guess, truer
to a world grotesque with human misery,
  where, as Flannery O'Connor

said about the deformed half
of everyone, the good in us is always half-
  completed and under

construction. Of course,
it's not a sign at all—just a junkshop curio,
  a cross of fishbone I've kept

for years on the mantle
in my study. I'm learning slowly to admire it
  for what it is: a stripped-down

bone curved where the brain's
blueprint of fluid motions once was harbored;
  a network of beautifully

dovetailing pieces created by
chance and function which, when it's taken up,
  has the cool patience of a shell,

the ocean's raw, clean smell.
If it says anything at all by not speaking,
  it's *fix your eyes on finitude,*

  the only path to wholeness—it is
  what has been given to you.

Two

Pompeii

How lovely and radiant they were,
the bride and groom, mugging
for each other before the ruins.

A photographer arranged them
face to face, a silhouette
shot, that appropriated the beauty

of two market columns and the view
they framed of Vesuvius which,
distant, illumined by the sunset's

elaborate orchestrations of roses
and violets, seemed airbrushed
of its past. Just that morning

we'd seen the bodies, renderings
in plaster of those lives
that stumbled and fell, leaving

their forms printed in
the nameless history of rock
as the mountain overtook them.

There was a man who must have seen
what was coming then buried
his head in his hands, and a woman,

lying face down, her body raised
slightly on one elbow and knee,
as if listening for someone who called

her by name. How young
they were, that husband and wife
of no more than an hour,

their happiness so casual and full
of the gaudy excess of the sun's
rich bands of light, it lifted

us toward them and, for a moment,
we followed them arm in arm
out the gate to where their limo

waited before we went our way,
wandering again along the tracks
left by wagons in the cindery streets.

Fashion Shoot, Frijoles Canyon

Where did they come from?—suddenly, among the Anasazi
ruins: two models, a photographer, two hair stylists,
a smiling entourage. Racks of dresses and skirts,
of blouses and vests and accessories. Across the canyon,
in the emptied rooms of a pueblo, I had been pretending
to piece together dusty traces of the past. I couldn't
imagine the effort required to cut dwellings out of cliffs.
I watched them through binoculars: flutter of hands,
sweep of skirts, a loose blouse luffing in hot breezes—
and the faces, changing expressions as the photographer
moved right then left, as he kneeled and lay down,
the rest following, as if wherever the models were going,
desire would be satisfied. He waved his arm
and the wind covered or revealed a face, the sun imparted
its fashionable radiance and shadings, and soon enough
I imagined the pages of the magazine taking shape,
its glossy attractions like a vague desire enlarging itself,
each new item turning into a necessity, its cost
and possession always larger and more elusive,
and always promising a greater satisfaction, the glory
of a different future alive in those clothes, in those two
models who went on posing long into the afternoon
in a world where the Anasazi scratched deer and running
men into the million-year-old canyon walls and then
vanished, leaving us to ask all these years, where did they go?

The Artist of Pontito

After they left, nothing was
the same. His mother's walnut bureau—
with her hairbrushes and combs and perfumes,
with its mirror where he'd look

at himself behind her
as she brushed her black hair—lay broken
and scarred, knifed with initials. The floors
reeked of stamped-in

cigarettes. Orchards
and fields were ruined. He was a boy when
the Nazis came. So many years ago, and
an ocean away now, but he

cannot stop remembering
the hillside above the stream where women
carried laundry on their heads. He can smell
the sun in a basket of sheets.

But he cannot see the women
when he lifts his brushes to paint the houses
and streets that hover in such detail he needs
only to trace the geometry

of tiered roofs, the odd angles
of hillside, street, and house. Pontito—
so much returns still of the old village:
the roadside by the west gate

and the gravel path that curved
behind the rectory; the view of the piazza
from his friend's house. But he cannot see
    the old woman who gathered

herbs, or the two village priests,
nor even the small gatherings of young men
and women who would sway in the shadows
    of the hotel awning. He has not

been back, but he paints every detail,
each window and door accurately placed, each
and every stone rendered. Thousands of canvases,
    his labor of over thirty years—

Pontito, his childhood home,
so peaceful and still, its streets strangely
empty, no one leaning out a window, no one
    to answer a knock on a door.

Blind

Between 1982 and 1989, nearly a hundred
and fifty Cambodian women in middle age
presented themselves to doctors in California,
and said they couldn't see.

Some can make out shadows,
some can count the fingers of a hand
held near their faces, some
see nothing at all. There is nothing
wrong with their eyes.

One starts a sentence and loses her way.
One looks like someone who hopes
she will not be noticed.
When she speaks, her hands fly up
in front of her face without control.
One hopes for rage or sorrow,
but the days repeat and repeat, each day
one that has already passed.

Doctors tell them: you must let go
of your memories. The women ask:
Where would they go?
They say no matter how
many things we forget, what happened
there is still so clear,
our lives now seem imagined.

What they see: a child
swung by his ankles, his head slammed

into a truck door. Then again, again,
again. A pistol. A small, unreal hole
in the back of a head leaking blood.
The bowels of neighbors,
fly-ridden. A sister, a husband, a child,
each day another death unburied.

The women say less and less,
using smaller and smaller words—
a language of the unsaid.
They drink tea, make offerings
to ancestors so that they will visit
their dreams, nap, wake, and sit
at their windows. Vague shapes
of cars and buses go by. They look out,
eyes drawn like shades against
the light. People go by without faces.

For Primo Levi

Since then, at an uncertain hour,
That agony returns,
And till my ghastly tale is told
This heart within me burns.

from Coleridge's The Rime of the Ancient Mariner,
Levi's epigraph to his last book, The Drowned and the Saved

What can they think?—
She was meant to live? She wasn't.
And yet here she is, before them,
a girl staggering to her feet
as if saved, her naked body imprinted
still with the press of the dead
that lay tangled over her—
the only one who has ever risen up
off the cement they hose down
after each gassing.
They wrap her in a blanket,
give her a chair to sit in, hot broth
to sip, astonished by the flush of blood
reddening her cheeks, by her eyes
that open and close, sunstruck
by the light on a field beyond
the window, light which could be
a new beginning but is not

in this story that Levi tells
near the end of his life.
No, the SS officer must be called,

and what choice has he—hasn't she seen?—
a man who cannot abandon a judgment
that is always final. And Levi?—
a year after trying to save this girl
from a second death
in the steady erasures of time,
he threw himself down a stairwell,
his body broken and twisted,
though daily, for forty years
after the camps, he had gone on
trying to be true to the mess of truths
he kept wanting to arrange,
but knew he must not, knowing
the carnage of such choices
and judgments—*you over here, you there.*

And yet what word
does not perjure itself? What words
advance a truth that is not
immediately *convenient?*
For forty years he wrote, but what
possible ending for this story
that circled like a noose,
always returning to the knowledge
that no one would live in his words.

Attending

Just the smallest of deaths
in a world riddled with deaths.
Death without a sign
of death, this array of sparrows
carefully dressed in tiny caps,
in hand-knit sweaters and scarves.

Not something the artist
could have foreseen
when she stepped on a sparrow
lying in a Paris street
and knew at once she had to care
for what was already beyond care.

Encased in a glass box,
this tableau of five rows,
six preserved sparrows to a row—
Boarders at Rest, the artist calls it
half-jokingly, as if we've just
peered behind the door

of the local shelter at the ones
we failed by our disregard,
at rest now finally
in their bundled sleep.
So peaceful, they catch us
off guard, and we feel

the sudden stab of the ironies
we've cultivated to explain
our indifference. And if we try
to look for the whimsy
in these too colorful caps,
the wink in these lidded eyes

which says, *the joke's
on death*, we cannot dispel
the charm of these
individually-sized sweaters
and caps, each one attending
so lovingly to a common sparrow,

an act so excessive and absurd,
and yet so natural,
it has kept us spellbound
this last hour,
and helped to bring us back
from our long, equivocal wanderings.

Bearings

Even near the end, his days full
of loose ends, of misremembered names
and frayed words that fed exhaustion,
he struggled, once or more a day,
to wake from sleep's long hours
of dispossession, his cancer-riddled
brain groping for words clear and exact
enough to bring back the familiar
and ordinary. *Where am I?*
he'd ask, and his wife, herself lost
in the ongoing displacement of all
they had, would begin the slow search
for language that might stay the inevitable.
Do you recognize anything? she'd reply.
Yes, that chair is like one we have at home.
You are at home, she'd tell him,
repeating the word until it focused
the room in his sight. Once or more
a day, they'd talk like this, painfully
adding one word to another, as if
living depended on the difficult saying
of what was meant. Yet, even at the end,
words would gather in a flash again,
connecting moments of grace and pleasure—
the house they rented once in Mexico,
the sun milling around in open-air rooms,
and the way sometimes their flesh
had broken open in each others' arms,
unburdened, permeable, voluptuous—

though those moments were no more
predictable than others that came
unbidden, the loss of one of their children,
his brother's death in the war, the night
his own chute opened above him like some
angel unable to prevent his slow fall
toward the mapless fields and trees
where the enemy waited, nameless
like himself, and perhaps like him,
saying the words of some prayer for
a moment's peace to get his bearings.

Against Consolation

The lecturer is talking
about Weil's essay on "Detachment."
The scent of lilacs
intoxicates the air inside the room,

cut branches brought in
to represent the flowering outside,
spring flaring up
again like those beliefs, I imagine,

Weil warns against—
beliefs which fill up voids and sweeten
what is bitter. A thousand
miles from here, you have given up

belief in the providential
ordering of events. No proverb sweetens
your suffering. What endures
is your bewilderment—the freakish

wheel of that truck
breaking off and hurtling through
the sunlit air, not enough
time to say *Look out* or even *Shit,*

before it struck
your car, one of hundreds lined up
in rush-hour traffic
on the other side of the highway.

You told me, the more
you think, the less you understand.
        You can't explain
the roof caved in all around you,

        your two friends buried
under metal, and you, who sat alongside
        them, untouched.
Home from the hospital, your friends

        dead, you went to
the kitchen, and everything, you said,
        was just as you left it,
as if the accident were only an interruption

        in daily life, a tornado
that leaves a kitchen table set for dinner.
        The contradictions the mind
comes up against—these are the only realities:

        they are the criterion
of the real. Weil again, who believes
        we come to know
our *radical contingency* only through

        such contradictions.
We must suffer them unconsoled.
        "Let the accident go,"
your friends tell you, "Don't hold on"—

        what we say, I fear,
to rid ourselves of the pain we feel

when your pain closes
in on us. It's late in the afternoon

and the rustling
of feet and papers has begun. I look out
    the window—a gusty wind
polishes the morning's rain-washed glass

of air, and the late sun
lavishes each new green with its shine.
    I'd like to dismiss Weil's
haunted, unnerving life as my colleague

quickly does, the lecture
ended: "Brilliant, but crazy." Anorexic,
    psychotic, suicidal. Labels
that fit, I suppose, and yet I cannot deny

the stark attraction
of her words. *Stay with your suffering,*
    I've heard her say
over and over today, always the extremist.

The last time I saw you,
I knew you lived at the border of what is
    bearable, that you'd seen
the skeleton underneath all your thought,

everything stripped
of sense or summation; you knew
    your friends' deaths
would make no more sense in time

and you would have
to live in that knowledge—no, not
          knowledge, the word
itself a kind of consolation, but the void

          Weil speaks of,
where you cannot escape the skewed
          wheel of a truck, the blood
on your hands, the voice you still have

          that calls out, *O God, no,*
the scent of lilacs that pierce the air
          each spring for no cause,
beautifully innocent of meaning.

Dust

Now when priests and faifthful say the words
life eternal no representations appear at all.

Czeslaw Milosz

Not John's new Jerusalem rising out of Babylon,
its whore become a bride, newly clothed in light;
not that city's gold brighter than the sun
where one timeless day banished the night

and a branching tree flourished beside a river,
its ripe, healing fruit extended to those
who sing the word's music on both sides of the water
without memory of lives that came to a close.

Not Dante's wheeling rose of ingathering light,
its perfection of form calling us from our wandering,
from our days of earthly exile and imperfect sight,
each returning step a remembrance and a forgetting.

Nor Luca Signorelli's vision of muscled eloquence,
death's skeletal body given its resurrection
in the perfect symmetry and quick intelligence
of human form leonine in its new dominion.

Not even Keats' earthly paradise of a *finer tone*,
time set aside in the sun's afternoon contemplation
of a bowl of tranquil blue grapes, each misted one
breathing in the light's final satisfaction.

No, we're finally certain that every revelation
is the result of circumstance and need—as today
on CNN, when callers tied up lines at the station
to say they saw Christ himself in the star-ridden gray

photographs sent down by the Hubble telescope. The face
of Gene Shalit came to others. Or the Statue of Liberty.
The *heavens?*—vast yet mappable stretches of space
where we monitor the accidental birth of some new galaxy

or posit a star's dark collapse amidst dark matter.
Where nothing exists because there is no observer.
Now, at odd moments, we feel the terror of dust's
new meaning: there is, of course, nothing more than us.

Gratitude

In his prison letters, Bonhoeffer is thankful
for a hairbrush, for a pipe and tobacco,
for cigarettes and Schelling's *Morals* Vol. II.
Thankful for stain remover, laxatives,
collar studs, bottled fruit and cooling salts.
For his Bible and hymns praising what is
fearful, which he sings, pacing in circles
for exercise, to his cell walls where he's hung
a reproduction of Durer's *Apocalypse*.
He's thankful for letters from his parents
and friends that lead him back home,
and for the pain of memory's arrival,
his orderly room of books and prints too far
from the nightly sobs of a prisoner
in the next cell whom Bonhoeffer does not know
how to comfort, though he believes religion
begins with a neighbor who is within reach.
He's thankful for the few hours outside
in the prison yard, and for the half-strangled
laughter between inmates as they sit together
under a chestnut tree. He's thankful even
for a small ant hill, and for the ants that are
all purpose and clear decision. For the two
lime trees that mumble audibly with the workings
of bees in June and especially for the warm
laying on of sun that tells him he's a man
created of earth and not of air and thoughts.
He's thankful for minutes when his reading
and writing fill up the emptiness of time,

and for those moments when he sees himself
as a small figure in a vast, unrolling scroll,
though mostly he looks out over the plains
of ignorance inside himself. And for that,
too, he's thankful: for the self who asks,
Who am I?—the man who steps cheerfully
from this cell and speaks easily to his jailers,
or the man who is restless and trembling
with anger and despair as cities burn and Jews
are herded into railroad cars—can
without an answer, say finally, *I am thine*,
to a God who lives each day,
as Bonhoeffer must, in the knowledge
of what has been done, is still being done,
his gift a refusal to leave his suffering, for which,
even as the rope is placed around his neck
and pulled tight, Bonhoeffer is utterly grateful.

After an Argument

We're in separate rooms, dark coming on
this day toward the end of summer
when clouds look as if they might unfold
into pre-fall cold, and a hummingbird flashes
at the window, then darts off, perhaps for good.

I'm straining to hear a Bach cello piece
you've turned too low, the two of us
retreating to the comfort of our own opinions.
I'm tempted to interrupt our quarreling silence,
to say how Simone Weil (the book in front of me)

compares the soul's relation with the divine
to two prisoners in adjoining cells.
It's true that each of us fumbles blindly,
eyes blocked by our own desires. Or we knock
against that which divides us as we try to look

with reverence on the other. We can lie
in bed back to back, like mirrors turned
to the wall when someone dies, that thinnest
barrier become a distance we cannot cross.
But Weil knew the wall separating two cells

is also the one means of communication.
Right now, what's left of the day arrives
in little shiverings of light that cavort
around the room, making windows on a wall.
When I get up to look out at the world

outside I've been following in shadows,
I see the same stand of tamaracks you'd see
from your adjacent room. Hallucinatory
and familiar in the watery air of dusk,
they groom the afterlight in their topmost

feathery branches—such unfazed, casual
beauty through which the day lingers on
and then is gone. I don't know
if you're looking at them, or if you would
feel as I do, lightened, grateful even,

as though a sickness had found its way
out of my body, but I'd wager you've felt
how such moments can lead us back
to the common world restored in our sight.
I was going to tap out an SOS on the wall

that divides us, but now, the dark flooding
from the corners of our rooms seeming to
enlarge them, perhaps each of us, the wall
our rudder, could drift into the arms of the other,
everything understood, nothing yet spoken.

Three

Kafka and the Rabbi of Belz

Rain for days and rain again tonight,
but the Rabbi's followers have taken to heart
a moment three days back when the Rabbi
emerged for his daily exercise and the rain halted
and the sun, as stories already have it, blazed again.
Kafka has tagged along, invited by a friend
who has told him how, when the Rabbi speaks,
everyday objects take on subtler forms.

By the swollen river, the Rabbi stares
so intently at the moving water, Kafka's friend
feels the Rabbi transferring the world into himself.
Kafka watches a swan that never once turns
its head, the bird utterly complete in itself,
inconvertible. It glitters in a circle of lamplight
then disappears under a stone bridge, an interval
passing so quickly it might never have been.

Gusts of wind make the flames in the gaslights
spurt and sputter as if any one of them, or all,
might break into speech. Piles of dead leaves stir
and are lifted up, weightless and figured
for a moment, before dropping to the rain-pocked
street. Above, the trees gesture mutely. The Rabbi
invokes Ezekiel, God's breath entering the bones
of the dead so that they stand up, alive again.

Kafka tells his friend the leaves are just leaves,
and this is quite enough for him.

On the walk back, Kafka sickens himself
with thoughts of work he should be doing,
has not done. When he looks down
the empty streets smeared with rain, the city
appears, as if through the wrong end
of a telescope, to be shrunken and abandoned.

A few days later, to his friend's bewilderment
and surprise, Kafka returns to follow behind
the Rabbi and his students. As they walk,
the sun dissolving over the city grants
the streets and buildings another, brighter life,
every edge gleaming. The Rabbi is talking
of what is sacred in every human being—
the sense, despite all odds, that life itself is good.

Kafka finds himself recalling a single paragraph
he wrote over and over, how it shone
unexpectedly with what he could not say,
the words enlarged, it seemed, by what was
uninterpretable, defiantly other, yet
requiring words. When his friend asks why
he has come, Kafka shakes his head and says,
there is always something unaccounted for.

Sunlight

What I wanted to do was to paint sunlight
on the side of a house, a roof . . .
　　　　　　　　　　—Edward Hopper

And so he wandered through
worlds that rose up and disappeared
in his rear-view mirror: fleeting

patches of red roofs and white
clapboard gable ends and windows
that reflected the passing light

and clouds and the moment
when the clouds cleared.
He saw himself in houses

at the edges of fields
and railroad tracks, in doors
opened on the sun-drenched

absence of vacant rooms;
in all those figures
behind lighted windows,

who gaze into the distance
or at nothing at all,
suspended in reverie or loneliness;

who are always waiting
at entrances
of buildings pressed together

in twilight shadow;
or on stoops and porches,
or in a room empty of everything

but the bare walls and a bed
where a woman sits, half-dressed,
a nearby window letting in

the morning light which moves
freely in its first clear brilliances.
The light shadows

the back of her neck, an arm,
touches her upper thigh,
but she remains impassive,

her hands crossed beneath her
knees. The window goes on
making a bright rectangle

of the sun on the wall beside
her, a silence through which
she might move, a door

of light which keeps extending
the luminous vacancy of morning,
a clarity without answers.

Passages

Called out of sky
burning toward ash
and evening's overtaking,
they appeared,

first in twos
and threes, and then
in small helixed flocks
that pivoted

together all at once,
as if some small flame
lights the dark
skulls of birds

with the most intimate
knowledge, complete
and present
from the beginning,

of a place
they cannot see,
but must go to,
along paths

at once apparent
and invisible,
flyways
millions of years old.

They were, I know,
only what they were—
cedar waxwings—
that called from

the wayside hawthorns
and ate their fill
of berries.
And their coming?—

only the flight
of birds as one
season ended
and another started again.

Still, as I went about
my work among the stone walls
and the flower beds
beside the old house

and the birds went on
with their flight,
it seemed that both of us
were living out

old claims that bound us—
to stay and to leave—
in the same light
of the same hour

that had come
and gone every year
and would again,
for all time, a single moment

I had passed through,
and recognized
by my passing,
my place in it.

Water-ouzel

Never shall you hear anything wintery from its
warm breast; no pinched cheeping, no wavering
notes between sorrow and joy; his mellow, fluty
voice is ever turned to downright gladness . . . .
                                        —John Muir

Across the century's divide, we look,
you and I, at the water-ouzel
that matches its flight to the creekbed's

windings—once the path of a glacier—
then touches down and walks casually
from one existence into another,

a door opening in a rift of dark water,
the bird flying now under water that rushes
over its head in the light and shade

of streamside cottonwoods.
For you, the natural world offered itself
in parables to whoever had ears to hear,

and the song of this drab, stubby,
wren-like bird never failed to cheer you.
On this cold, glum February morning,

it cheers me too and I can almost hear
why you heard its near unceasing song,
despite the weather, as praise

for its maker, birdsong and water
shelving from rock to rock.
And yet it's that *almost* which fills me

with unease. Isn't this bird
so drolly dipping its squat body
in the cold stream almost insignificant?—

not God's emissary in this
unthinkable century, but the true naif
of rushing water and waterfalls,

blithely singing as the world shatters
and regroups around its head.
Still, like you, I can't take my eyes off it

as it goes on doing what water-ouzels do,
up to its neck in water one moment,
singing under a waterfall the next.

And, if nothing more, it reminds me
that not everything is about the tropes
we make of it— as you knew

better than me, I suppose, your own joy
mostly in walking through a world
full of capricious loops and detours

where we can stop for awhile
under the cloud-darkened sky, and be
refreshed by a bird's sunny antics.

Natural History

(Corkscrew Swamp, Florida)

Like some speeded-up parable of creation,
the solid sky dissolves in fluid greens
and silvery blues, in flares of lightning,
heaves of thunder and plunging dark,
the storm coming in as we stand here,
fear and exhilaration nesting in us
as hundreds of vultures and storks,
invisible just moments before, climb
a swirling ladder of winds, their helix
appearing and disappearing in shifts
and tilts of light, the ladder rising
a thousand feet, the spiral of birds
only the barest glimmer—then gone,
as if they've entered some ark in air.

First, the pull of currents made visible
in the swamp and a skink circling
the railing of our small open-air shelter,
its roof humming with rain. Then,
a snake fitting itself to a cypress
rooted in water and, as in a dream,
dripping leaves that breathe frogs
and salamanders. From time's beginnings,
a pair of gar fin the new shallows,
at home already in the still rising water.
We sit without speaking, as if language
had returned to wind in the trees,
to spider webs of fern and leaf,
to the sibylline rush of rain.

Moths

I woke to the flutter of all
their wings over the screen
as, slowly, they assembled
themselves out of the dusty
half-light of morning—
thirty-four moths,
their small grey-brown bodies
covering the screen like lichen.
At noon, they basked
in what little sun there was,
the pale September light
resting briefly on wings
that moved hardly at all
yet never stopped moving
until the moths began
to die. Even then they
seemed more composed
than exhausted, taking
the time they needed,
as if they were dreaming
their death into being.
They simply became their end,
death so naturally wrought,
I needed to touch each one
to be certain. Where
I placed my finger, they broke
out of their bodies
in little puffs of dust, leaving
behind an imprint

on the screen. By then
evening had entered
the day, and the sky, dense
with saturated colors,
collapsed in on itself,
the low clouds igniting
in a bonfire of last light.
And I felt suddenly
the slow, irreversible moment-
to-moment urgency
of every thing to keep
moving—and I leaned close
to the screen and blew
my breath on what remained
until nothing was there,
then stood a while listening
to the wind in the leaves
while the plush dark freed
a scattering of stars and the moon
broke clear of the trees.

Last Things

His children came as if their own good health could restore
his. He lost a little more each week, the tumor taking
his legs and then the memory of what just happened
moments ago. Still, he made not walking as matter-of-fact
as walking, found jokes in his forgetting. "Hello," he'd say,
picking up the phone, "You've just reached Bob's
Brain Tumor Clinic, leave a message and he may or may not
get back to you." How quickly he learned to help them again,
as if, as their father, there were these last things to do.
When pain flashed in his eyes, then drained away,
his children could see how their wanting him, even as he was,
would give them no peace. When he slept, they watched
him move inside his dream as if he were mapping
the circumference of everything he was taking leave of—
the newly planted weeping cherry just outside
the front door, the crocus and daffodils he forgot
the names of, and further off, the city he loved, bodiless
clouds skimming its horizon of buildings. Near the end,
papers came and went with the daily news, and faces,
each becoming another and another, flowing past him
like leaves on a childhood river. Half in delirium, he'd speak
of someone he couldn't see who kept coming for him.
Before he went, he waited for his children to come and say
goodbye. And when he was gone, they gathered
around him, and looked into his face, and touched the scar
on the back of his head where the tumor divided
the father they knew into bits and pieces. And each of them
found they had the strength to lift and hold his head
in their hands one last time, its weight the size of a world.

For a Friend's Baby

We've come, neighbors and friends, to this high crown
of field to watch for *shooting* or *falling* stars, their name
depending, I guess, on what we bring to this hill.
Our friends have brought their new child and place her,
face up, on a blanket under the night sky. There's the usual
naming of what little we know—Big and Little
Dippers, Cassiopeia, and the stars we think are Perseus—
and then we settle in, timing flights out of Hartford,
a steady pulse of red lights tracing roadmaps
on the sky, this one going West, that one headed out
towards the ocean bustling with its own lanes
of dark activity. Near midnight, and my ten year old son
is on his feet, announcing *there's one*, and sure enough,
the sky's come alive with its white torch. Soon,
meteors arrive as quick as we can count, streaks of light
too quick to hoard, the profligate sky tossing
a bright profusion of starry coins over our heads
until we're all shouts and smiles. Afterwards, I think
of how the gods loved Perseus and helped him
defeat Medusa. And the story's other half—the discus
he threw that killed his grandfather by accident,
none of us able to escape the harm we'll give
and receive. Hannah, these are times when stars
are mostly falling and nothing godly visits.
There are no messages in these stony particles
that burn in our air, nothing occult in this August
night; there are only these meteor showers

that have occurred before, over and over, and will
occur again, and the ordinary moment of our meeting
which so improbably breaks us open each time
into such sweet happiness, as you did, upon your arrival.

The Day After Viewing an Exhibit of 17th Century Dutch Paintings

I'm doing errands, thinking about a hip,
ironic best seller in Japan—a manual
(*Complete*) for suicide—the author's flip

voice casually laying out the choices: a lethal
jump from a building or in front of a train
which, he'll have us believe, can be pleasurable,

like freezing to death once you've chosen
a cold night, and wet your body with water.
Sit back, relax, be patient. To quicken

the process, have a drink: the author
assures, there's rarely any anxiety or pain
and, if you're bored doing the same thing over

and over, *why not* choose another option.
It's pretty much the same if you live or die,
Japan's under 30, what's-the-point generation

reasons. Here, *life sucks and then you die,*
our bumpers announce more succinctly.
I've shopped, mailed the bills, stopped by

the cleaners. Now I'm parked aimlessly
along the new river trail. A few ducks
paddle up to a child for bread, entirely

unafraid. It's lunchtime and the trucks
of local tradesmen pull in, church bells
count to twelve and stop, and two hawks

idle above the river that still swells
with spring run-off. The good luck of a day
that slows us down, gives us a chance to revel

in blues and greens, forget what's held at bay:
a sick child, a close friend with cancer,
a marriage that's lasted for years, but may

fall apart at any moment. No wonder
the Dutch devoted so much attention to
the everyday. And, if their subject matter

has lately been discredited (what's true,
the newly rich in love with possession),
those painters who worked so minutely knew

in detail how soon we come to our end,
and how much effort it takes to build
a house where that daily constellation

of events—laundry, cooking, milking, field-
work, and the pile of bills that must be paid—
are part of the light in a glass half-filled

with wine, the late afternoon sun rayed
across a river meadow, the otherworldliness
of two children, their concentration stayed

on a risen house of cards as darkness
starts to seep into the room and emerge.
Patterned carpets, maps, those cross-

points of doors and halls and that wedge
of light that nimbuses a hand holding
a letter or a face lost for an age

in a moment's thought: each astonishing,
as simply to be living is. Homer knew
the choice is always between something

and nothing. He gave Achilles two
options—a short heroic life or a long,
unremarkable one. In Hades, Achilles knew

all too well what was lost to dying young.
Life ends, he tells Odysseus, who, like us,
doesn't yet fully understand death's song

is silence. *Don't tell me life is precious,*
the manual mocks, *we're all powerless.*
Yes, how quickly these unearned days pass.

Sam Cooke: *Touch the Hem of His Garment*

As if he cannot help himself
from adding up what's lost to the good times
   so difficult to have in this world,

   Cooke's throaty voice warbles
up out of his reed-thin, man-child body,
   half-balm, half aching need,

   his trademark whoa-ooh-oh-oh-oh
lingered over, drawn out until it hangs in air,
   honey-tongued, heavenly, fragile

   as consolation. I'm listening
to a 1956 recording, and Cooke, twenty-five,
   has already discovered his gift

   for making women tremble
and shake with the spirit in church aisles.
   He's retelling the Gospel story

   of a woman who wants only
to touch the hem of Christ's robe, a song
   that will sell twenty-five thousand copies,

   propel Cooke into a gospel star,
and begin the long chain of small decisions
   that ends with a bullet in his lungs.

Still eight years away—
the $3-and-up motel, the hooker charging
    assault, Cooke's cherry red Ferrari

    purring in the parking lot
as he slumps to the floor, naked save for
    an overcoat and one expensive shoe—

    but I can't keep from hearing
the urgency in his voice as the woman, pushed
    by the terror of self-recognition,

    her flesh dying from the inside
out, staggers through the crowd around Jesus,
    and, with only the slightest brush

    of her fingers, touches
his robe, believing it will make her whole.
    Who has touched me? Jesus asks,

    and Cooke sings, *It was I-I-I,*
extending the moment in his clear, sustained
    yodel, pulling us into the miracle

    of how, after night-long drifts
from bar to bar, the slur of zippers and
    whiskeyed words dimming the nameless

    landscapes of a hundred
identical blackened factories stuck between
    billboards and railway bridges,

after a week of days piling
one on another like dirty laundry, Sunday arrives,
    and everyone rises and testifies

    and sways under the wings
of notes that swoop and glide and make us whole,
    if only for the duration of the song.

Pause

(for Robert)

A teenager now, already it's hard
for you to feel more than the practiced
ironies and diffidence, too many
hours already spent pretending
you've seen it all, and repeatedly.

An hour ago, I dropped a book
and it fell open to this—*only chance*
can speak to us. I thought of Picasso,
of how he found his sculpture of a bull
in the odd conjunctions of a rubbish heap,

an old bicycle seat lying near
a rusted handlebar becoming the bull's
head. I don't know if chance spoke
to Picasso, or why thinking of that
happy accident led me to the night

you were born. Your mother's water
had broken and, driven by worry,
the hospital two hours off, the road
fogged-in and narrowed to what
our car lights could dimly map,

I almost drove over a baby rabbit—
a distillate of rain and moon-shot fog
that formed suddenly out of mist,

and brought us to a standstill.
Your mother and I just sat there,

forgetting ourselves and where we were,
as slowly, and a little at a time,
the rabbit became solid and actual:
first the alert, twigged ears diamonded
by rain-lit mist at each hair's tip;

then the downy, crescent-shaped body
poised on those nimble-muscled feet
created for feints and dartings.
So vulnerable and yet so completely
at ease—only a rabbit, it took all

our attention. As we sat there,
we began to hear what was happening
around us—the sluice-rush of water
in a nearby brook and the fainter
background simmering of raindrops

in a fuchsia hedge touched by wind.
Even a dog barking and the ping
of rain on the car's metal roof
seemed a completely new language.
I can't explain why one incident

triggers another or why, together,
they become something else entirely.
I'd like to call it the plenitude of
the unintended. The truth is,
I don't know if chance speaks or if

the mind just cobbles together whatever
it needs—but this world is full of
accidental moments that can stop us
in our tracks and wake in us again
the strangeness we were born to.

NOTES

"Elegy for Chris McCandless": The facts in this poem were taken from a *New Yorker* piece, "I Now Walk into the Wild," by Chip Brown.

"The Artist of Pontito": This poem is loosely based on the story of painter Franco Magnani as told by Oliver Sacks in the chapter, "Landscape of His Dreams," in Sacks' book *An Anthropologist on Mars*.

"Blind": The facts in this poem were taken from a *New Yorker* piece, "A Changed Vision of God," by Alec Wilkinson.

"Attending": "Boarders at Rest" is the work of Annette Messager.

"Against Consolation": The title of this poem comes from a passage by Simone Weil in her essay "Detachment": "Human misery would be intolerable if it were not diluted in time. We have to prevent it from being diluted *in order that it should* be intolerable. . . . We must not weep so that we may not be comforted."

"Kafka and the Rabbi of Belz": Kafka's walk with the Rabbi of Belz is referred to in Peter Mailloux's biography of Kafka: *A Hesitation Before Birth*.

ACKNOWLEDGMENTS

Grateful acknowledgment is made to the following journals, in which these poems were published:

American Literary Review: Mappings
American Scholar: The Purse; Nests
American Voice: Fashion Shoot, Frijoles Canyon
Boston College Magazine· Pause
Boston Phoenix: Distances (as At the Nursing Home)
Chelsea: Natural History
Dark Horse Literary Journal: The Artist of Pontito
DoubleTake: Sam Cooke: *Touch the Hem of His Garment*
Green Mountains Review: Kafka and the Rabbi of Belz;
    For Primo Levi
Image: Between Worlds (as Pause)
Kenyon Review: Against Consolation; In My Study
Ontario Review: Attending; Bearings
Orion: Elegy for Chris McCandless; For a Friend's Baby
Paris Review: Gratitude
Poetry: Self-Portrait; Narcissus; Gift
Sewanee Review: Dust; Questions
Southern Review: After Viewing an Exhibit of 17th Century
    Dutch Paintings; Blind; After an Argument; Water-ouzel
Southwest Review: Pompeii
Tar River Poetry: Passages; Sunlight
TriQuarterly: Moths; Last Things

Dust was reprinted in *And What Rough Beast, Poems at the End of the Century*, eds. Robert McGovern and Stephen Haven, Ashland Poetry Press.

Sam Cooke: Touch the Hem of His Garment was reprinted in *The Best Spiritual Writing* 1999 ed. Philip Zaleski, Harper San Francisco; *Kafka and the Rabbi of Belz* was reprinted in *The Best Spiritual Writing 2000*; *Gratitude* was reprinted in *The Best Spiritual Writing 2001*.

Gratitude also appeared in *The Pushcart Anthology: Best of the Small Presses*, Pushcart Press, 2002.

Gratitude; Fashion Shoot, Frijoles Canyon; and *Moths* were reprinted in *Poets of the New Century*, eds. Weingarten and Higgerson, Godine, 2001.

Sam Cooke: Touch the Hem of His Garment; Against Consolation; Self-Portrait; Between Worlds; and *Gratitude* were reprinted in *The Breath of Parted Lips: Voices from the Robert Frost Place*, Volume One, CavanKerry Press, 2001.

I'm grateful to the Connecticut Commission on the Arts for a fellowship that supported the completion of this book and especially to the College of the Holy Cross for a faculty fellowship and sabbatical during which most of these poems were written. And many thanks to a number of friends for their comments: Joan Sidney, Brad Davis, Bill Wenthe, Bob Deppe, Jeannie Braham, Christopher Merrill, and especially Gray Jacobik and Jeffrey Harrison. And finally thanks again to Shirley Adams for her help in preparing this manuscript and for her example of strength and courage in the face of great pain.